Copyright © 1991 by Dieter Betz
American text copyright © 1992 by Tambourine Books
First published in Danish as *Bjørnefamilien* by Gyldendal
An international coproduction arranged by Gyldendal, Copenhagen

Library of Congress Cataloging in Publication Data

Betz, Dieter, 1940–. The bear family/by Dieter Betz;
photos by Dieter Betz.   p.   cm.
Summary: Describes the lives of grizzly bears living on a game
reserve on the McNeil River in Alaska.
1. Grizzly bear—Juvenile literature.   [1. Grizzly bear.
2. Bears.]   I. Title.
QL737.C27B45513 1992 599.74'446—dc20 91-42698 CIP AC
ISBN 0-688-11647-7.—ISBN 0-688-11648-5 (lib. bdg.)
10 9 8 7 6 5 4 3 2 1
First U.S. edition, 1992

DIETER BETZ

The Bear Family

TAMBOURINE BOOKS NEW YORK

Alaska lies way up north. The Eskimos call it Alakshak—the big country.

The largest part is still wilderness. With active volcanoes, floating icebergs, and eternally snow-covered mountains, Alaska can be a harsh place to live.

Not many people can be found in most of Alaska, so the animals have lots of room. Wolves still prowl in the deep forests. Eagles fly high above the endless plains, while moose wander down ancient trails alongside the world's largest herds of reindeer. The lakes and rivers teem with countless fish, while walruses and seals sleep on black beaches of volcanic sand along the coasts.

But the animal known as the king of the wilderness is the grizzly bear.

The grizzly is a loner by nature. It marks its territory by making scratches on the trees with its sharp claws and by leaving its own smell on the ground. Other bears are warned not to approach too closely.

It isn't easy to come across any bears as they wander alone over such a vast area. But bears do have one weakness. They love salmon!

In the summertime, when the rivers are full of salmon, the bears forget for a while their need to be alone. They wander over enormous distances to take part in the annual salmon feast. Some of them meet in the reserve by the McNeil River, where they can be seen at close range, safe from hunters.

There are very few roads in most of Alaska, and in bear country there aren't any. And it's dangerous to reach the reserve by boat because of the uncertain weather and the many underwater rocks. The only way to get there is by seaplane, but the tides don't make it easy. The water rises and falls twenty-five feet every day in the bay where we have to land.

At high tide there is just enough water to let the plane land and drop us off by the beach. But the pilot has to take off again quickly before the tide starts to go out again.

Our tent is near the water's edge, but there's very little water to see right now. The tide has left the bay almost dry.

Larry, the reserve keeper, lives most of the year in a wooden hut nearby. He leaves only during the winter when the bears are in hibernation.

Larry knows a great deal about bears, and he is very fond of them.

Larry is armed. Bears can be dangerous if humans behave carelessly around them. But Larry has never shot a bear in the fifteen years he's been at the reserve, and he can't imagine ever having to.

At a distance the bears all look alike, but from close range they're as distinctive as human beings. Larry knows all the bears that visit the reserve. He has given them names to help keep track of them.

On the way down to the beach we meet Scarface. Old Scarface has fought lots of fights with other bears. When he came to the reserve he was already fully grown, so nobody knows how old he is. A grizzly can live to around thirty.

This is Romeo. When a bear feels threatened it rises onto its hind legs to detect any possible danger. Romeo has to be on guard and keep a careful distance from the older bears all the time. Being a young grizzly isn't easy.

We have to be careful never to disturb a sleeping bear. It can become very angry.

It's hard to identify the bear having an afternoon nap here. We stand very still, but the bear has already heard us. It's young Luther, and he sniffs the air to catch our scent. Bears don't see very well and have to depend on their fine sense of smell.

Fortunately, Luther shows no interest in us and goes back to sleep.

Groucho is out of breath because he has just chased away a cheeky young he-bear. Older bears don't like younger bears coming too close, especially young males. Young bears have to learn to respect the older ones.

Pretty Marie is six. Next year she will be old enough to have cubs. When she is ready to mate, maybe she'll meet an interested he-bear.

The adult male begins to look around for a female partner in the middle of the summer. But the females pretend not to notice the males.

At first, it's hard to tell if they are interested in each other. Male and female growl at each other all the time and both look very dangerous.

In the end they become friends, but only for a few weeks. Once they have mated, they separate. They may never see each other again.

A female bear brings up her young alone.

Virginia and Tim are brother and sister. Their mother left them last summer when they were almost three years old. By that age, young bears have learned to look after themselves.

Virginia and Tim have stayed together since their mother left, but now, in their fourth summer, they will split up.

Down by the river are both large and small bear tracks. The bears slide in the soft mud, but they don't fall because they have long, sharp claws to grip with.

And it's down by the McNeil River that we meet Teddy and her cubs. Teddy was only four months old the first time she wandered out of the mountains with her mother. She really looked like a teddy bear, so that's what Larry called her.

Now Teddy is eleven and has her second litter of cubs. It's hard to believe that this thousand-pound grizzly weighed barely a pound when she was born.

Imagine if a human baby grew that much!

Last autumn Teddy went high up into the mountains to find a place where she could be alone and in peace, away from people and other disturbances. She dug out a winter den in the mountainside. She shoveled with her enormous paws and put all her strength into sending the earth and stone flying down the mountain.

When she had dug out a narrow corridor, she made a cozy lair at the end of it and rested there after the exhausting work.

Soon the first snow blocked the entrance so that only a small air hole was left. Nobody could find the sleeping bear now. She was safe and warm in her thick winter coat.

In the middle of the cold, dark winter, while snow whirled wildly out on the mountain, Teddy gave birth to her cubs. They were blind and bald and looked almost like helpless baby mice. But it didn't take long for them to begin crawling around their mother's thick coat to find the place where they could suckle her thick milk.

For three whole months they did nothing but eat and sleep, eat and sleep. . . . Meanwhile, their mother snoozed away in the quiet, cozy den.

When the snow began to melt and the water began to drip down into her den, she knew it was time to go outside. Her cubs looked like real bears now, with thick coats and black, inquisitive eyes. Together with their mother, they were strong enough to wander out into the dangerous, exciting world.

It was hard for Teddy. After six months in the den, she was tired and weak. The only food she could find was roots and shoots and bark. She always had to be on guard for other bears that might kill her cubs.

One day she found a ground squirrel's nest. She dug so that earth flew all around her and, after a short chase, she caught the squirrel. It wasn't much for a great, big bear, but it was the first delicious mouthful she'd had after six months of sleeping through the winter.

On her way to the valley and the river, Teddy met a moose with two big calves. What a meal that could be! But moose are too fast, even for a hungry grizzly bear.

As soon as Teddy reached the mouth of the McNeil, she made a secure resting place for herself and her cubs. She dug a hollow on a grassy slope, down toward the sea. From here she would be able to see a hostile bear from far away.

Even though the cubs were always hungry, Teddy suckled them only a moment at a time. She was on constant watch for other bears who might think of attacking her or her cubs.

But even a bear can get tired!

Suddenly, a big he-bear surprised Teddy while she was resting. Teddy attacked immediately. Nothing in the world is as dangerous as a mother bear protecting her cubs. It was a fight about life or death and the growls could be heard far out over the bay.

Teddy won the fight and returned bleeding to her cubs. But one of them had disappeared! Frightened by the big he-bear, it had rolled down the slope and fallen into the sea. The current swept it away.

Teddy searched for her cub. For hours and hours she trudged up and down along the coast with her other cub at her heels. That cub became too exhausted to walk any longer. Teddy lay down flat beside it.

The tired cub crawled up onto its mother's back, and Teddy carefully got up again. The cub clung tightly to Teddy's thick fur. They had to keep searching for the cub that had drifted out to sea.

At low tide, something dark on the sandbar far out in the bay caught Teddy's eye. Quickly, Teddy swam out to it. It was her other cub!

Now it's summer.

Teddy walks restlessly up and down the riverbank, waiting for the salmon. They should come at any time. The salmon swim up the rivers from far out at sea to lay their spawn.

Teddy is hungry. She has to eat constantly to be able to supply milk for her greedy cubs. Since there aren't any salmon yet, she has to find something else to eat. Like all grizzly bears, Teddy eats almost everything, from roots, grass, and meat to sweet berries in the fall.

When she munches grass, Teddy looks like a big, furry cow.

One day the salmon arrive.

The bears are ecstatic and throw themselves around in the water trying to catch them.

Teddy's old uncle Waldo can't understand where his fat salmon has disappeared to. He'd just thrown himself right on top of it.

This time, he manages to catch it. He spears the salmon with his long claws to make sure it doesn't get away again.

More and more bears come to the river. They all want the best fishing spots and it's hard for them to keep a distance from each other.

Old Diver likes to fish in the middle of this waterfall. He often keeps his head underwater while looking for salmon, and he can hold his breath for an incredibly long time. Nobody knows how he manages to see the salmon in the gushing rapids, but he sure is good at catching them. Look how plump he is!

Another bear is teaching her young to fish in a little pool at the bottom of the waterfall. It isn't hard to see the salmon in the crystal clear water.

This little bear is called Julie. She is five years old but small for her age. Julie doesn't dare go down to the river when it's crowded, so she mostly eats grass. Could it be she doesn't like fish?

In the afternoon, when most of the bears are napping from their enormous feast, the river quiets down. Julie finds a place where the water is shallow, then lies down and takes a bath.

For a bear, life is a question of survival. The more it gets to eat, the more chance of surviving the winter. It has to make sure to get a thick layer of fat to be able to survive the six long months of fasting during hibernation. A grizzly can easily gain three hundred pounds during the summertime.

After a bear dives for fish, it has to shake the water off its coat. The thick layer of fat protects the grizzly against the cold while it stays in the icy water for hours at a time.

Finally, a bear gets so full that it can't force any more salmon into its stomach. Then it goes up into the forest to rest. Before it can fall asleep, it may have to dig a hole in the ground for its bloated belly. After snoozing for a couple of hours, the grizzly is ready to eat again.

A bear's life is mostly dominated by two things—eating and sleeping!

Teddy has to catch more than a hundred pounds of salmon a day, so she has no time to waste. The cubs grow quickly, but they can't catch fish by themselves, and depend completely on their mother.

Teddy is very good at fishing, but she is constantly having to chase away other bears. Teddy is extra careful and takes no chances.

But how can Teddy both fish and watch her cubs when there are so many other bears around?

Suddenly Teddy takes her cubs onto her back. Now she can take them out to fish with her. But they have to hold tight!

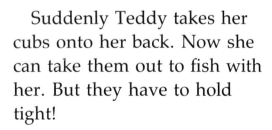

It isn't easy, though. The cubs don't hold on well enough and they keep falling in the water and getting soaked.

Too bad. Teddy swims ashore and puts the cubs down.

Teddy finds other bears dangerous, but she doesn't seem to know that people are the greatest danger of all. She's never met a hunter or heard a gunshot.

So one day Teddy chases another bear away, then walks right toward us with her cubs.

Larry whispers, "Keep quiet. Don't move. Don't panic."

Teddy stands quietly, looking at us for a long time. Then she comes a little closer. Our hearts beat faster, but we aren't really frightened.

What will Teddy do?

Teddy has come so close that we can hear her breathing. She rolls onto her back, grabs her cubs, and squeezes them onto her chest. While Teddy watches us with her small, intelligent eyes, we can hear the cubs suckling her milk.

As soon as the cubs are full, Teddy gets up and licks the milk off their black muzzles. Then she pushes them down into the grass, as if to say, "Stay here until I get back."

Without turning back, she goes down to the river to fish.

Teddy has left us to babysit!

One September morning everything seems different. The first night frost has enchanted the landscape. Now it's time for the bears to go hibernate. They'll have to wander far away from the safety of the reserve.

Some will never return.

But next summer the salmon will be back, and so, we hope, will Teddy and her cubs.

DIETER BETZ has traveled all over the world to photograph nature's treasures, including walruses in the Bering Sea, sea elephants in Mexico, and many unique species in the Galapagos Islands. Mr. Betz was born in Germany and has lived in Denmark since 1964.

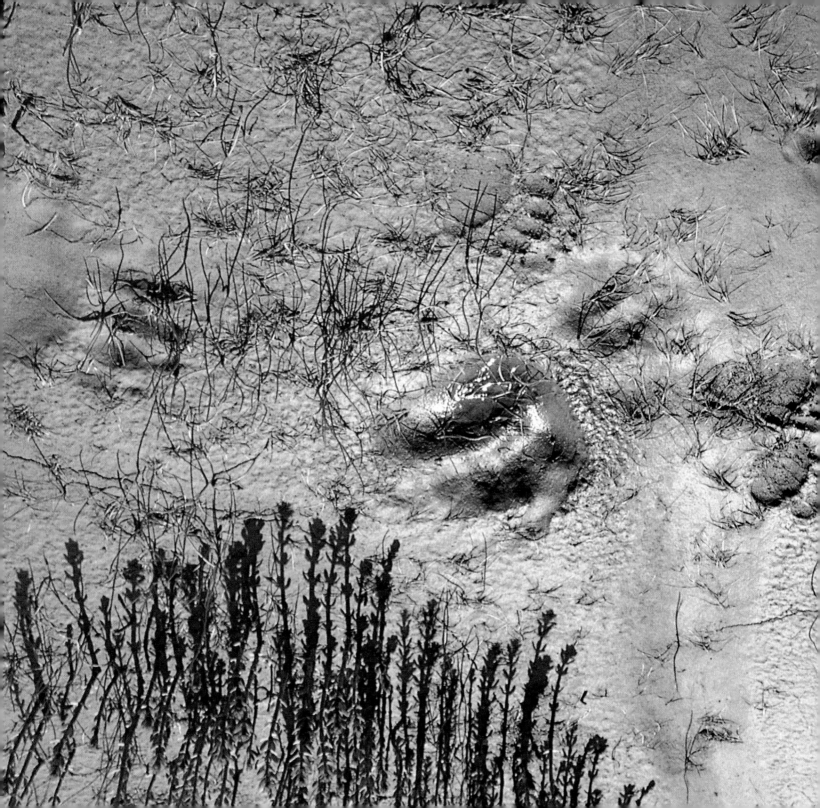